The Story of Saint Patrick

This story was adapted by author Ann Carroll
and illustrated by Derry Dillon

Reprinted 2017

Published 2013
Poolbeg Press Ltd

123 Grange Hill, Baldoyle
Dublin 13, Ireland

Text © Poolbeg Press Ltd 2013

ISBN 978 1 84223 593 5

Cover design and illustrations by Derry Dillon
Printed by GPS Colour Graphics Ltd, Alexander Road, Belfast BT6 9HP

The Story of Saint Patrick

Also in the Nutshell series

The Children of Lir
How Cúchulainn Got His Name
*The Story of Saint Patrick ***
The Salmon of Knowledge
The Story of the Giant's Causeway
The Story of Newgrange
Granuaile – The Pirate Queen
Oisín and Tír na nÓg
The Story of Brian Boru
Deirdre of the Sorrows
Heroes of the Red Branch Knights
The Adventures of the Fianna
*The Adventures of Maebh – The Warrior Queen ***
Diarmuid and Gráinne and the Vengeance of Fionn
Saint Brigid the Fearless
The Vikings in Ireland
Journey into the Unknown – The Story of Saint Brendan
The Story of Tara
Niall of the Nine Hostages
The Magical Story of the Tuatha Dé Danann

*Also available in Irish
Scéal Naomh Pádraig
Méabh Banríon Na Troda

Before sunrise the raiders swooped on the sleeping village, swords drawn. They forced the youngsters from their beds and killed any adult who tried to stop them. Leaving swiftly, they marched their captives to the nearby coast and set sail from Britain towards Ireland and home. Behind them was a scene of bloodshed and grief.

The captives were Christian teenagers and among them was Patrick, a boy who had known only a pleasant life with family and friends.

Now he was a slave, sold in Antrim to work
as a shepherd on the wild mountains and live in
a stone hut.

Every day he had to make sure none of the flock was missing or injured. He kept the sheep away from dangerous tracks and deep gorges. In winter he dug them out of snowdrifts and in spring took care of the lambing. It was a life without comfort.

Often he would think of his family and home. Often, especially in the freezing winters, he would ask God to help him escape.

Over the years he managed to learn the language and slowly he got to know others who lived on the mountains, some of them Irish, and would find his heart lifted by their music and song.

In the seventh winter he dreamed that God was calling him: "It's time for you to escape, Patrick. You must find your way to Wexford where a ship is waiting to take you home."

"But, Lord, if I'm caught I'll be killed at once!"

"Patrick, you've been looking to escape for seven years. Now is the time. Don't get caught!"

In darkness Patrick left the hut and made his way down the treacherous mountain. There was no moon and it began to snow. He grumbled to himself that God might have made it a bit easier, but then realised that in the darkness he could not be seen and the falling snow would soon cover his tracks so the slave-owner would have no idea which way he had gone.

In time he got to Wexford, found his ship and arrived home to a warm welcome.

In time, too, he had another dream. Now the voices were Irish: "Come back to us, Patrick, and tell us about your god!"

Patrick thought, I'm not going back to slavery. I'm not going back to those wild mountains and I never, ever want to see another sheep!

But the voices in his dream insisted, "Come back to us as a messenger from your god. Teach us about Christianity!" and Patrick found himself drawn.

He prepared well for his mission. He left
Britain and became a monk, studying throughout
Europe. He was made a bishop and at last, in
the year 432, Pope Celestine sent him to Ireland
with a small number of monks.

During his exile in Ireland Patrick had learned a lot about the Irish and he knew the most important person in the land – the man to impress – was the High King who lived at Tara

in Meath. So he and his group settled in nearby Slane and waited for Imbolc, or the Rites of Spring.

At the beginning of February every year the High King, Laoghaire, lit a huge bonfire on the Hill of Tara. This was a pagan rite which burned away winter, encouraging spring's new growth. No one else was allowed have a fire on that day, under pain of death, for it was believed that

any blaze started by ordinary folk would cast a curse on spring and then nothing would grow.

When Laoghaire climbed that morning to the summit of Tara to light a bonfire that reached to the heavens, he was amazed to see huge flames in the distance at Slane and turned to his druids in fury.

"Whoever has done this thinks he is as important as a High King! He must be challenged!"

The druids too were enraged and urged Laoghaire to find the villain who had shown so little respect and kill him at once.

So Laoghaire and his followers marched on Slane, a magnificent sight in their colourful robes,

rich ornaments, long hair and beards. They met
Patrick and his men, dressed plainly, with no sign
of wealth.

In spite of himself, the High King was impressed.
That such simple people would stand up to his might!
They must be special. And so when Patrick swore

his Christian God would allow nothing bad to come from the bonfire at Slane, Laoghaire wanted to hear more and invited him to Tara next day.

The druids instantly hated Patrick. They knew he would shatter their might. For centuries the Irish had been pagan, worshipping many gods.

There was a god of beauty, of fire, of courage, of medicine, of forests, of mountains, of land and of sea, and many more. For every part of life there was a god and the druids were their High

Priests. They were powerful and wise men with great influence at court and among the people. If Patrick succeeded, the life they'd known would vanish.

And when he came to Tara carrying the
Christian cross before him, the druids spoke
among themselves.

"We must stop him," they said. "He will
destroy the great festivals of Imbolc, Bealtaine,
Lughnasa and Samhain. He will banish the
gods we love and we will no longer be able
to contact our ancestors in the Other World. He
will ruin our traditions and we will be lost."

The High King saw how troubled the High Priests were and pitied them. Yet he respected this stranger who had shown such courage and he listened as Patrick explained, "There is only one Christian God and in Him there are three persons – Father, Son and Holy Ghost."

"Ridiculous!" said one of the druids. "You can't have three people in one person. You're insane."

Patrick spied a plant on the ground and picked a piece of it. "Look," he said. "One shamrock, three leaves. One God, three divine persons."

"Well, we don't like him! Our gods are bound to have greater magic as there are so many of them. See!"

One pointed to the sky and immediately the
sun vanished and heavy snow began to fall.
Patrick sighed and bowed his head.

At once the snow vanished and the sun reappeared.

"Magic!" the druids said.

"Miracle!" Patrick corrected.

"Magic!" spat the druids.

"Miracle!" insisted Patrick.

"Enough!" said Laoghaire. "My ways are the old ways. I love the ancient traditions and won't change. But I respect you, Patrick, and

your god. So you are free to travel the land and convert any who want to become Christians."

So Patrick and his group journeyed through the countryside and spoke to the people. Many were converted, especially when they saw the miracles the Christian God could perform.

Once when Patrick rose to speak to a crowd, he pushed his walking stick into the ground and immediately it grew into a living ash tree. This impressed everyone, for before nothing had grown on that land and this was a sure sign that from now on crops would thrive.

Another time when Patrick was in the West, a huge serpent slithered out of a lake and drew itself up to a great height, ready to coil around him and crush him to death. But Patrick seized a stick and with one miraculous blow the snake was dead. His blood oozed into the water, turning it red, and from then on it was known as Lough Derg, or the Red Lake.

His mission was such a success that when he was in Mayo he decided to spend forty days and nights alone, fasting on a mountaintop, giving thanks to God. From the summit he could see the Atlantic, at the edge of the known world, with nothing beyond except mile after mile of battering waves.

Suddenly he was no longer alone. From nowhere the snakes came, in their hundreds and then in their thousands. They twisted

over the rocks towards Patrick, giving him no peace, lunging, tormenting, attacking. His stick could hold them off for only so long.

They are evil, he thought. They want to destroy me and God's work. And so he rose from his knees and challenged them: "Let all the snakes in Ireland come to this place and do battle!"

The mountain became a writhing mass of serpents, the air black with their bodies. Patrick could no longer see the ocean.

Swiftly he prayed: "In the name of God I banish all snakes from Ireland, messengers of the false pagan gods. I cast all serpents into the sea!"

At once there was a great hissing sigh as the snakes turned away. The rocks and crevices of the mountain were bared once more and all along the Atlantic's edge the water boiled and foamed as they disappeared into its depths.

Down below, anyone who witnessed the sight would never forget it and they spread the word throughout the land. Thousands more became Christians and forever after the mountain was known as Croagh Patrick (Patrick's rick).

Eventually Patrick settled in Armagh. He died on the 17th of March 461, mission accomplished.

The old pagan ways disappeared, as did the pagan festivals, and in their place came Saint Brigid's Day, Easter, Halloween, Christmas and all the Christian feast-days.

Yet there are some who claim a ghostly fire still burns on Tara at the beginning of every spring. And the druids and their gods are not forgotten. They linger in folktales and on the edge of memory, part of the magic of the past.

The End

Available in the HEROES series:

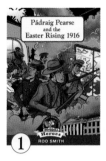

1

2

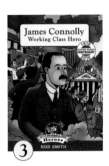

3

4

5

6

7

8

Available Now in Irish:

 ORDER ONLINE from poolbeg.com

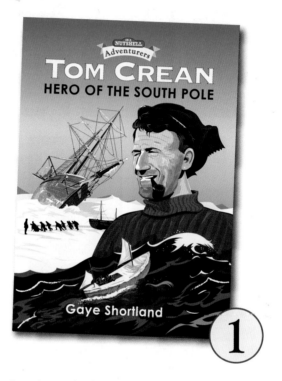

In 1918, sailors from the famous polar ship *Endurance* recorded a ballad about one of their fellow crew members. The chorus went:

Hail, hail, Tom Crean, hail, hail, Tom Crean,
He's the bravest man that the world's ever seen.
Hail, hail, Tom Crean, hail, hail, Tom Crean,
He's the Irish giant from County Kerry!

So who was this man hailed as a hero and loved and respected so much? Who "faced death many times and never backed down"? And how did this farmer's son from Kerry, who ran away to join the navy at 15, come to be such a famous Antarctic explorer? This is his amazing story.